AF265901

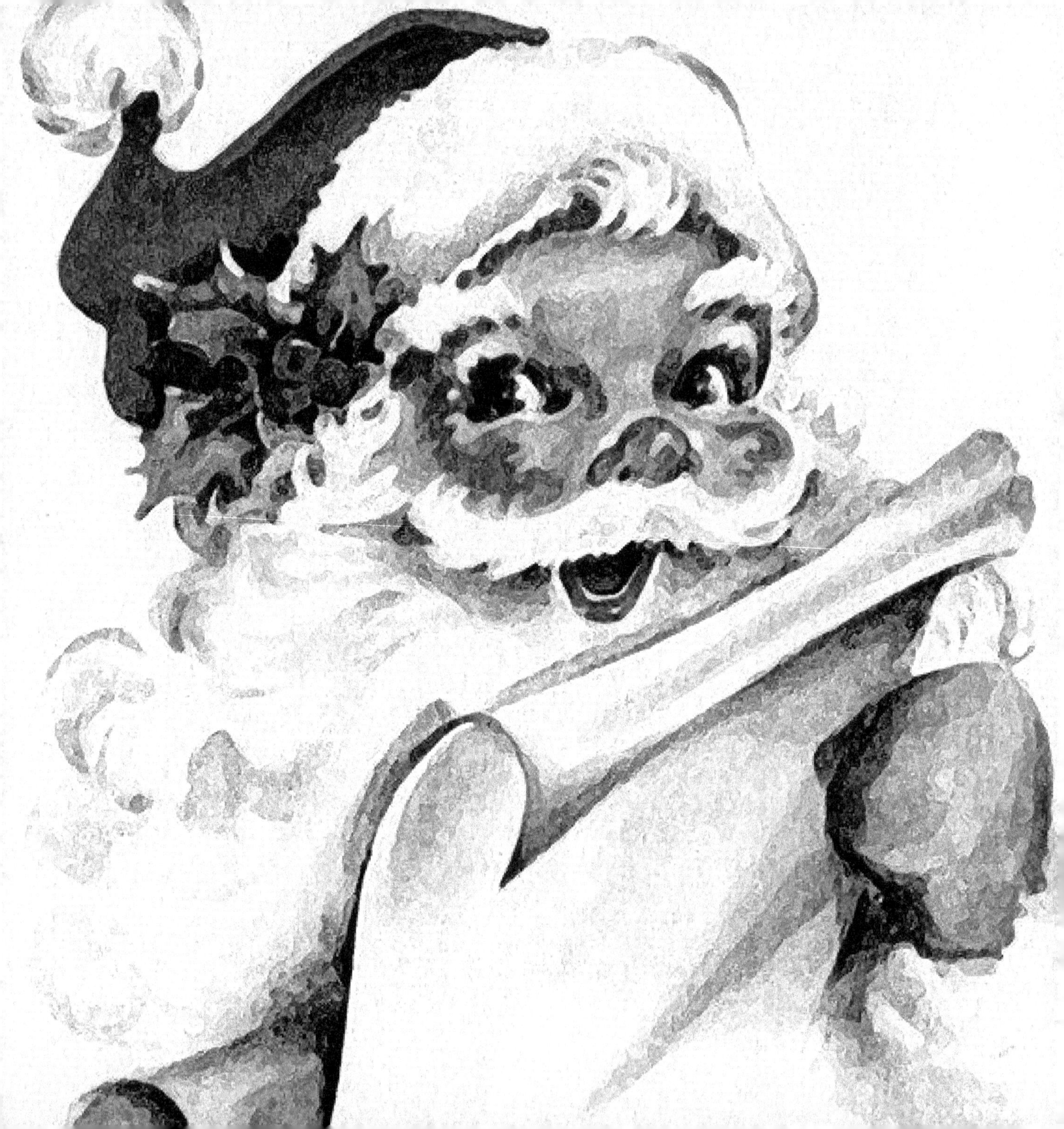

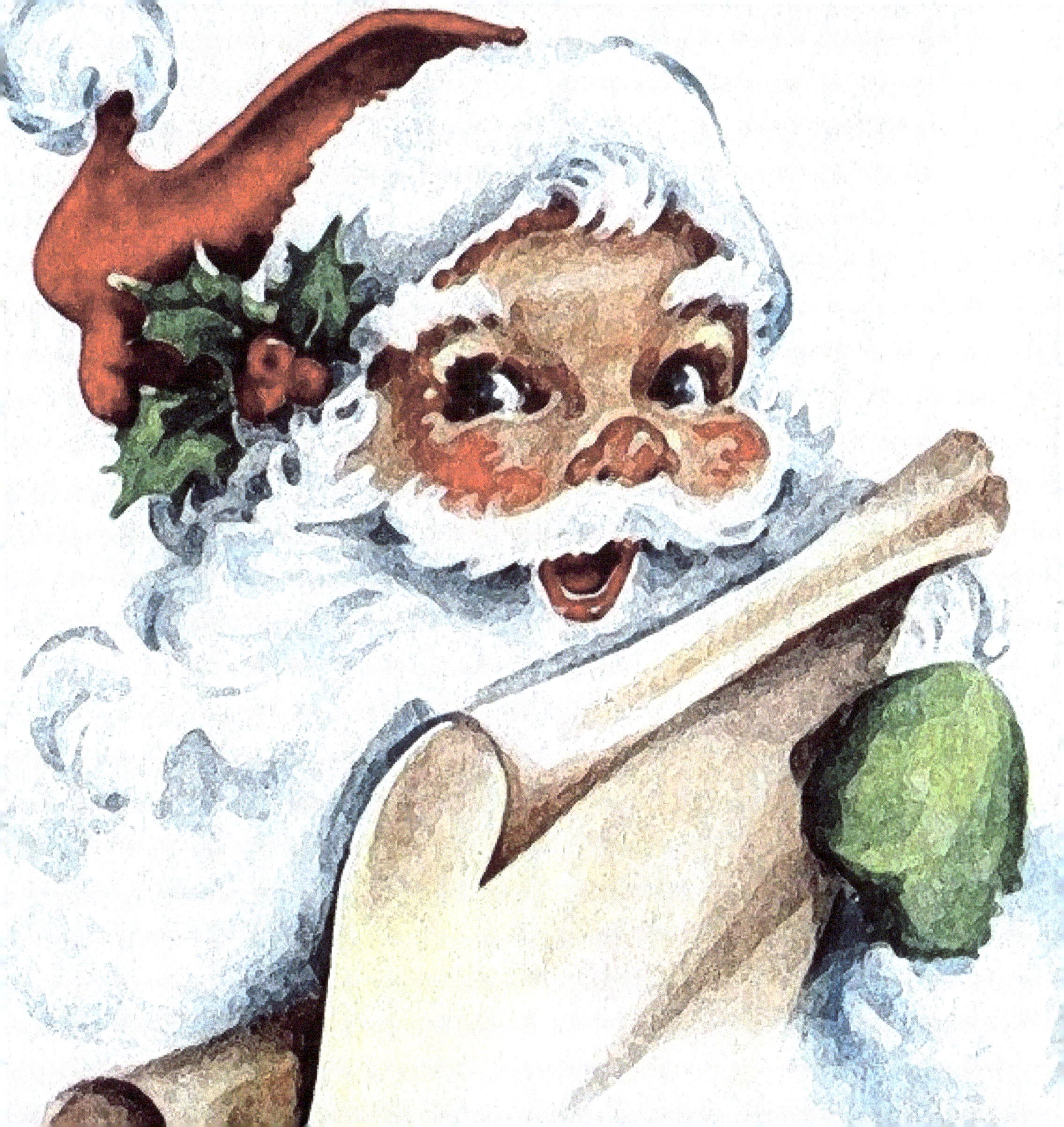

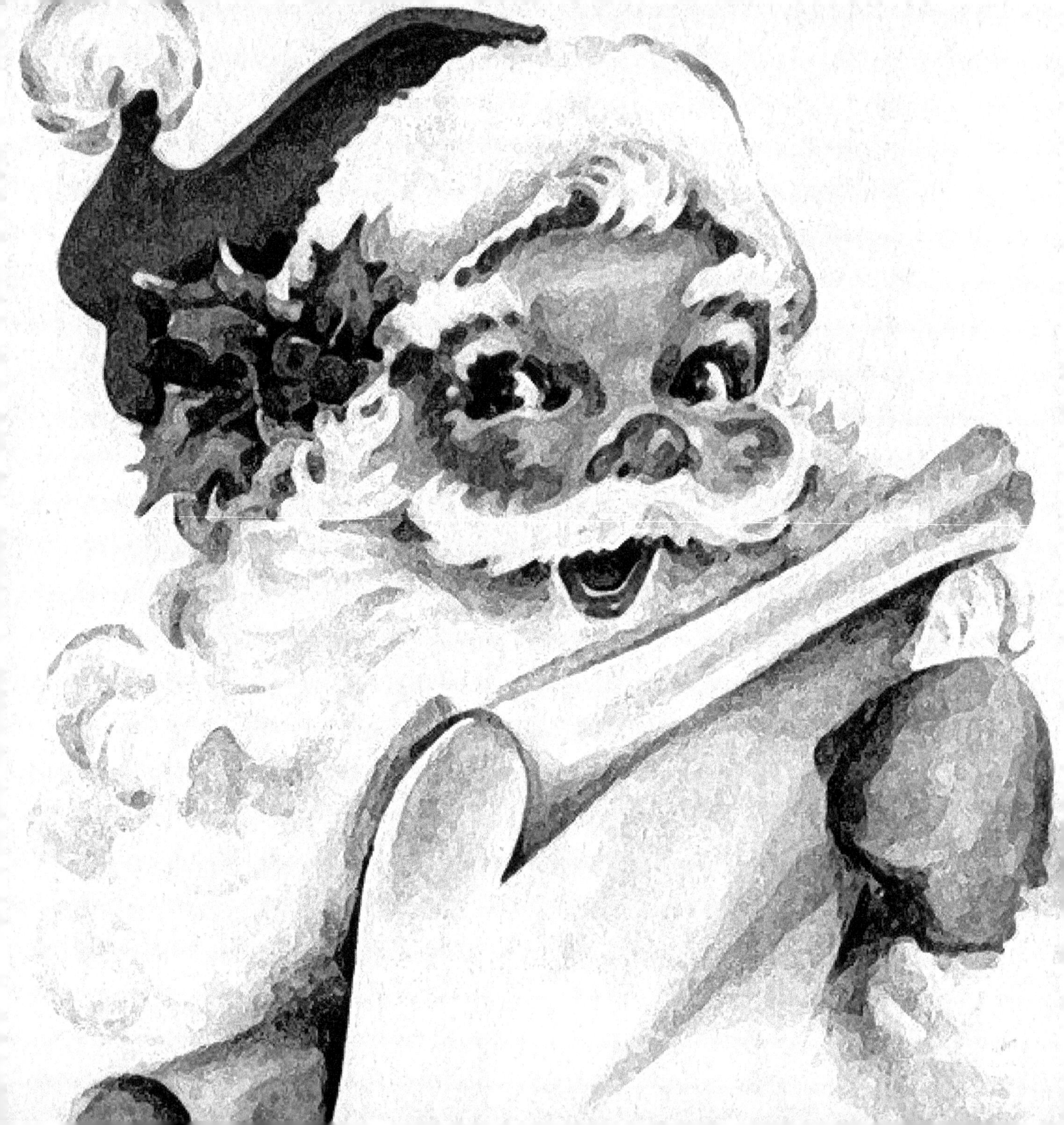

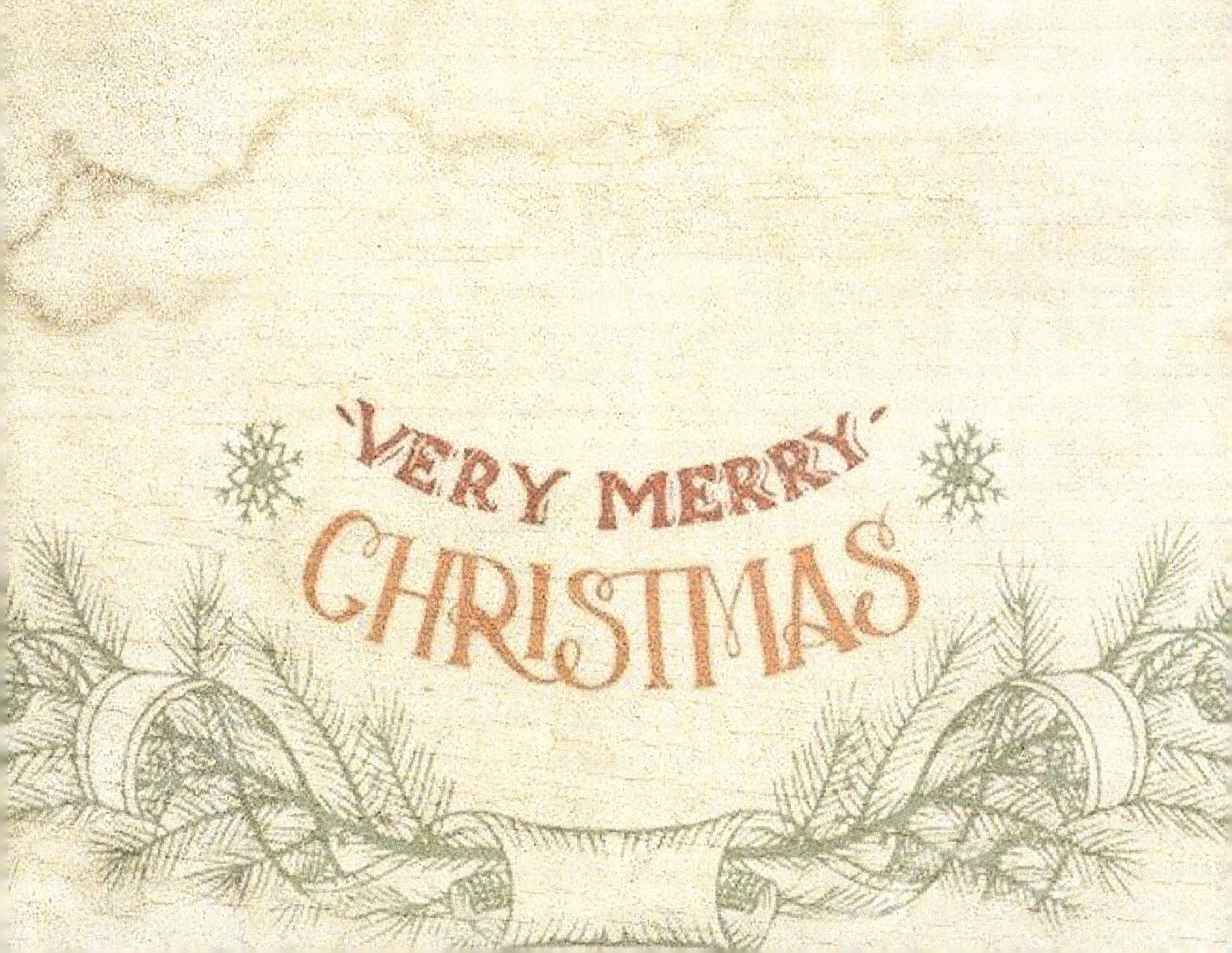

'VERY MERRY'
CHRISTMAS

VERY MERRY
CHRISTMAS

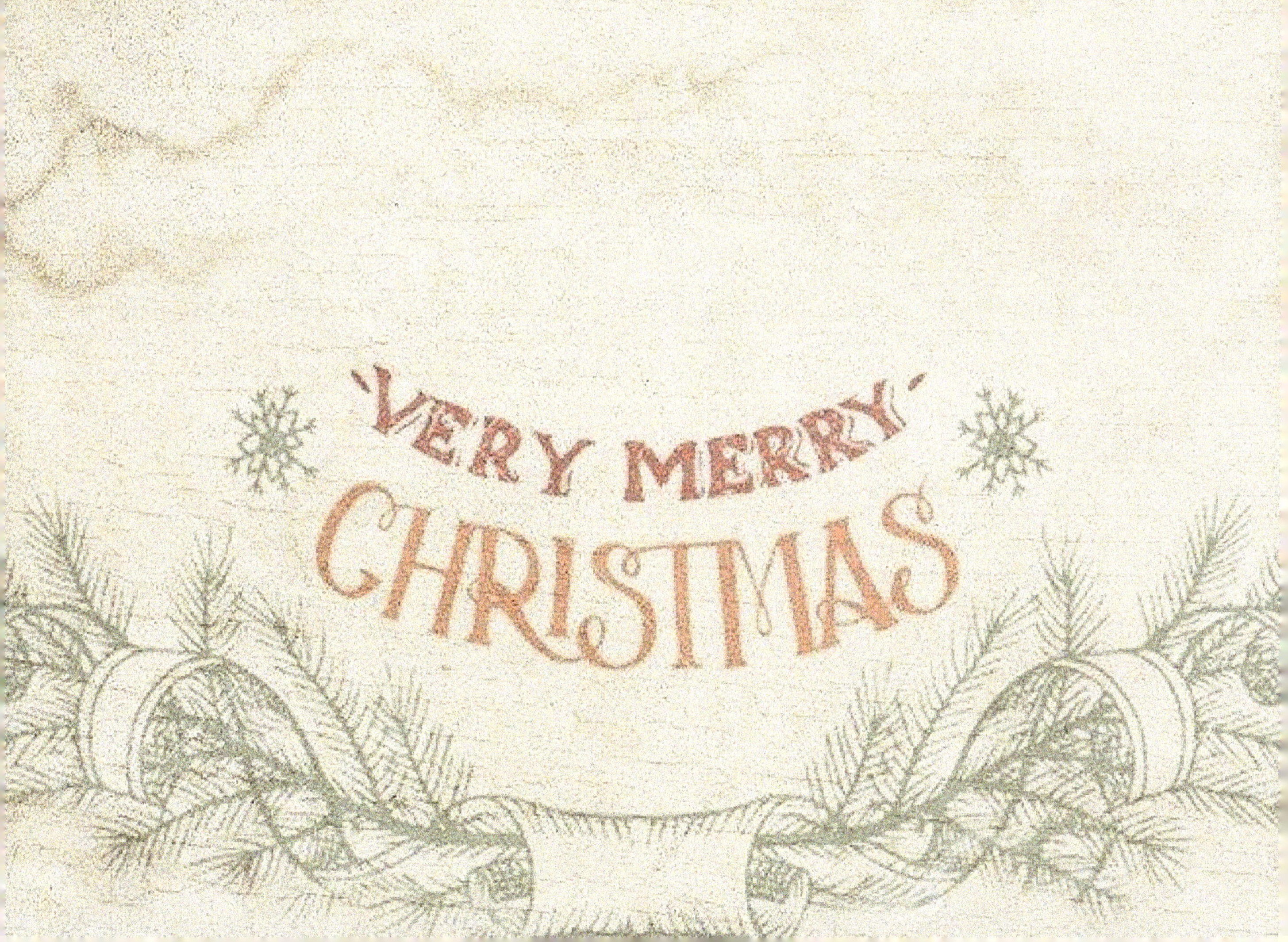

`VERY MERRY`
CHRISTMAS

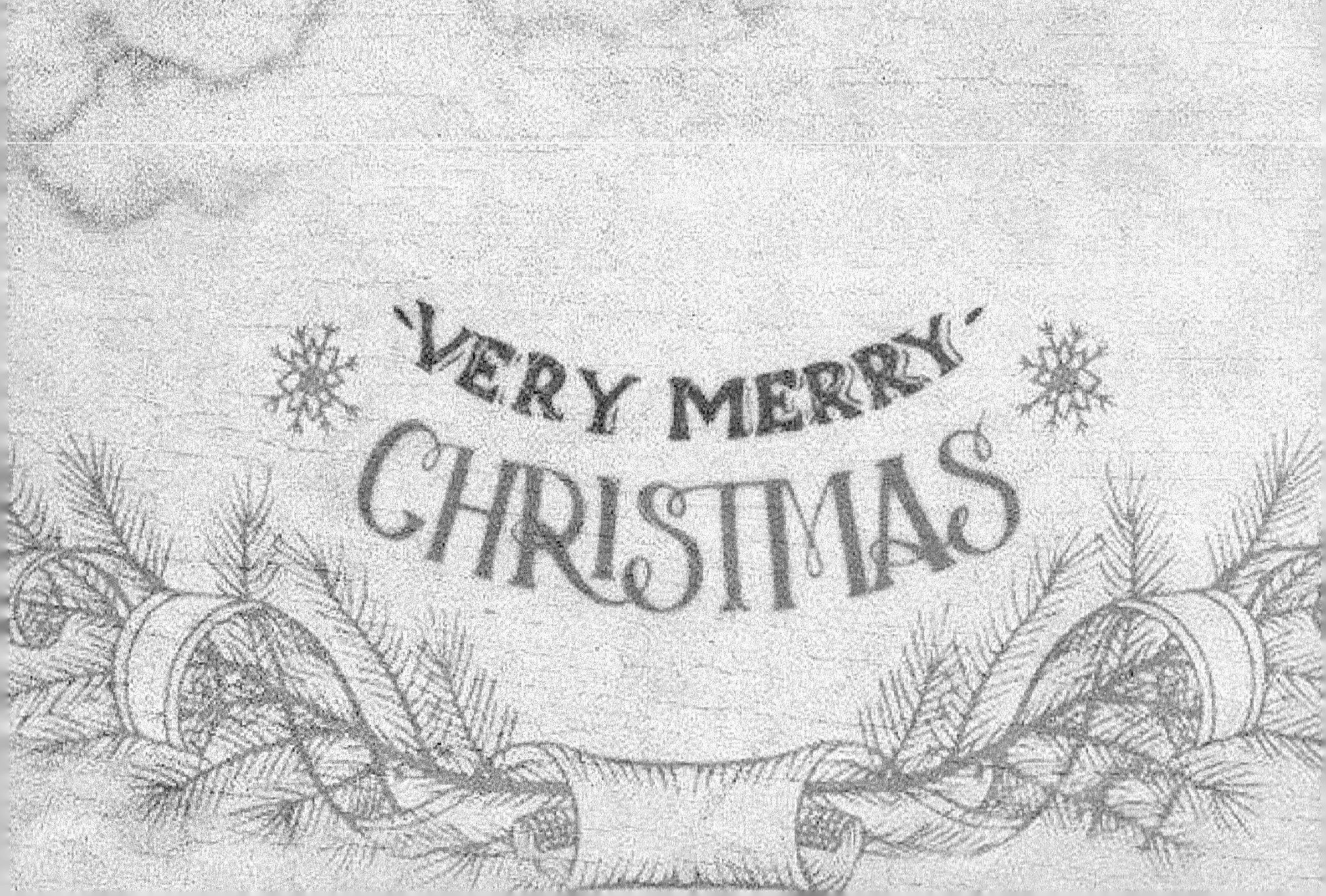

VERY MERRY
CHRISTMAS

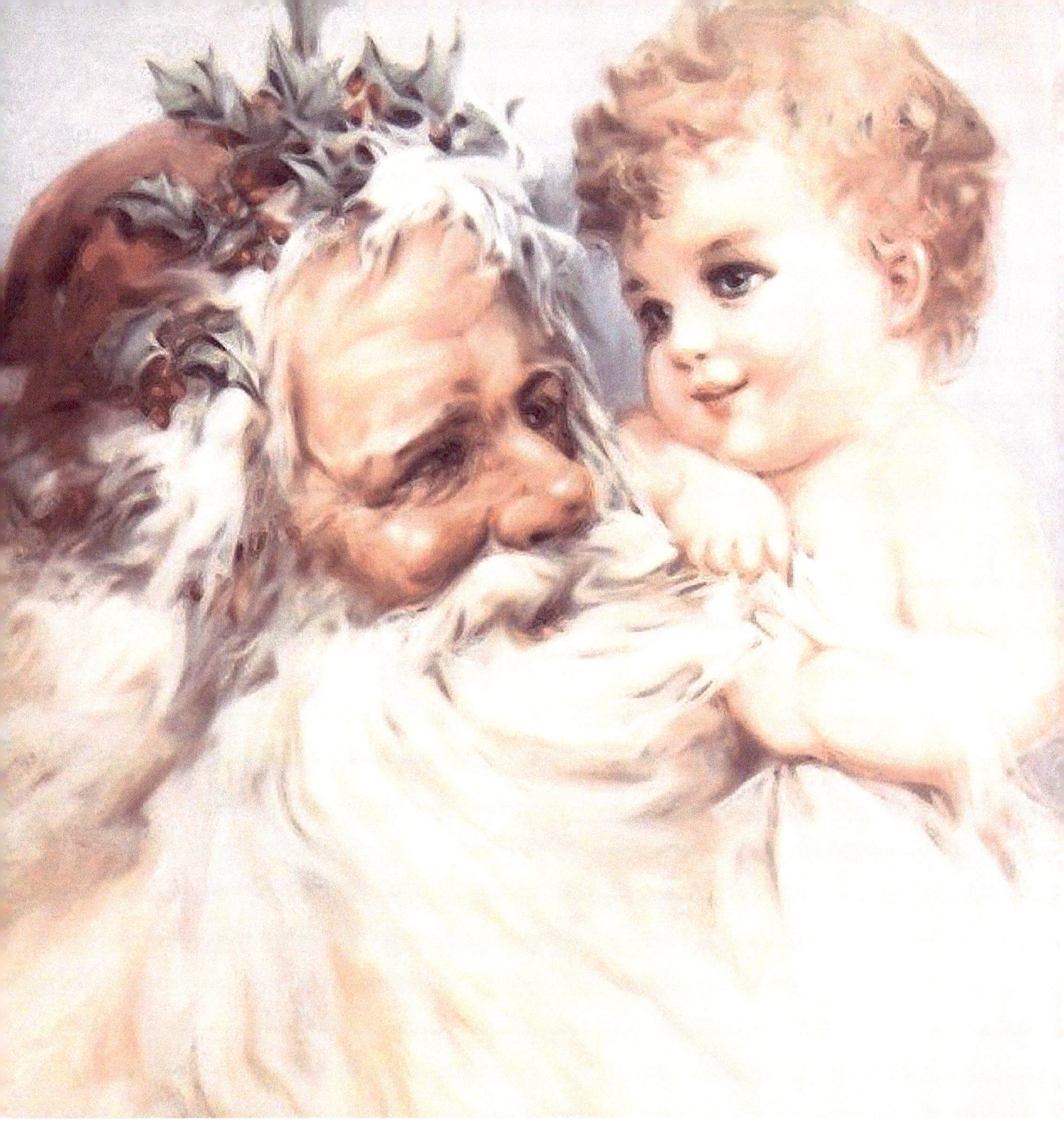

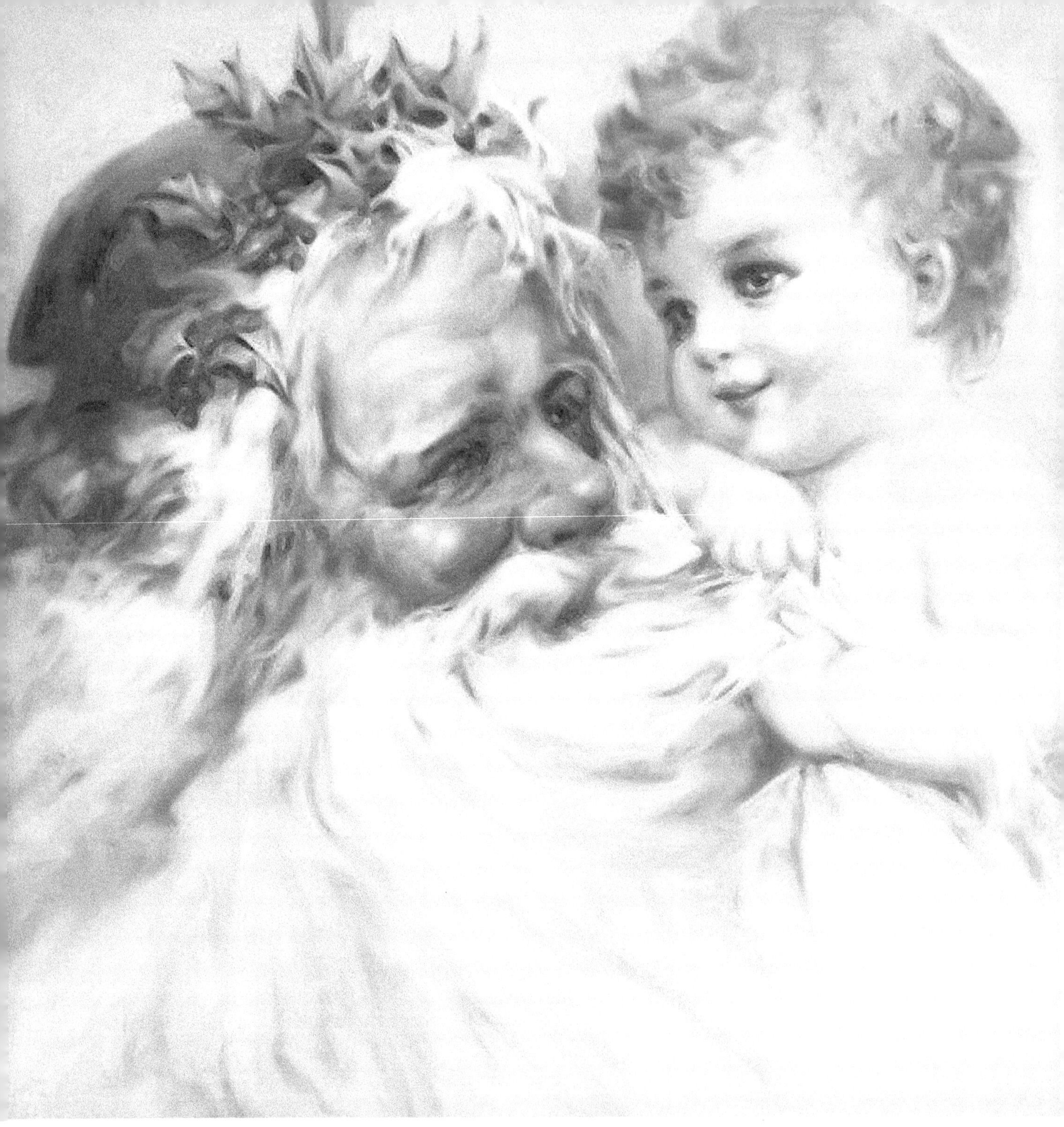

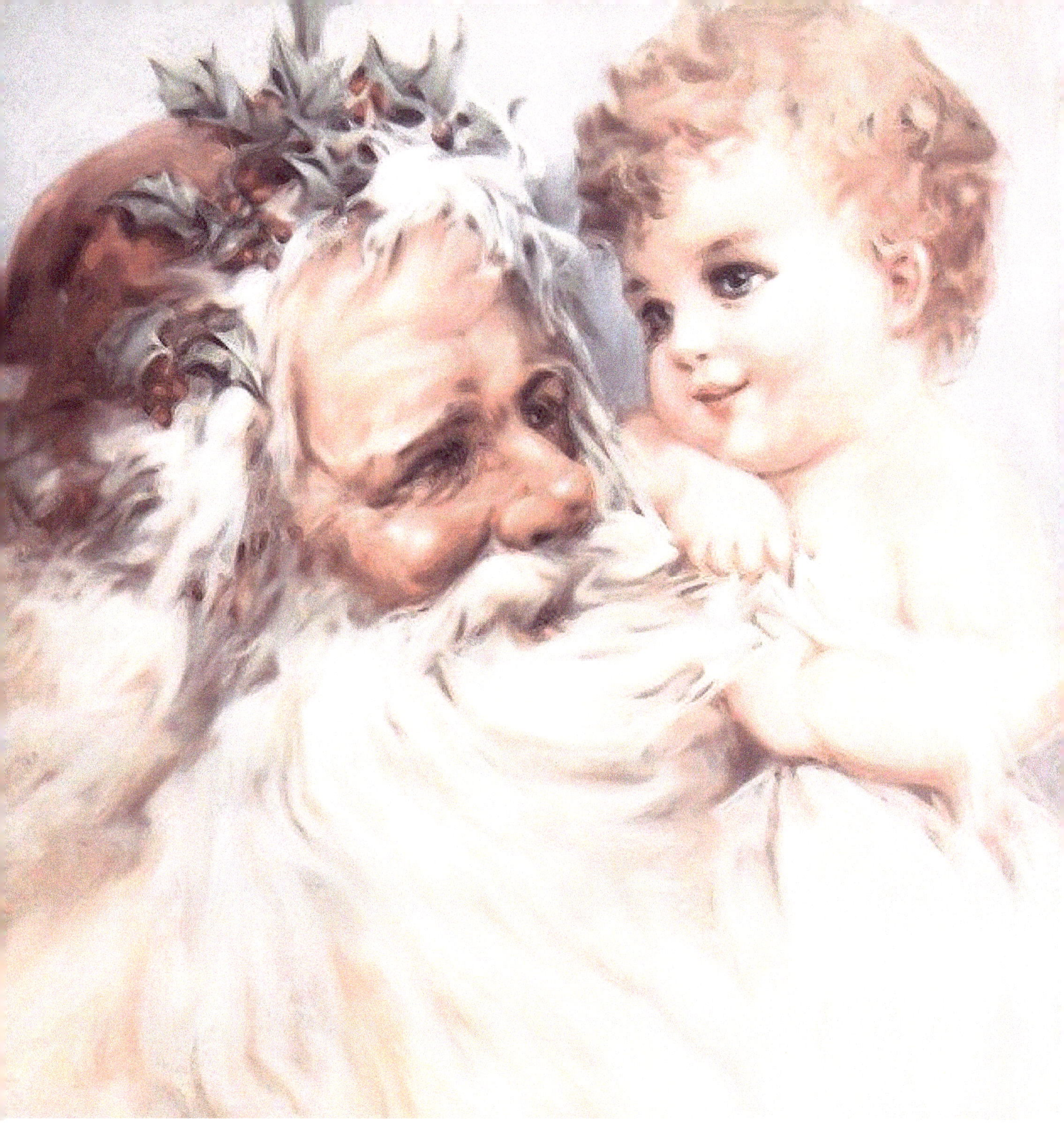

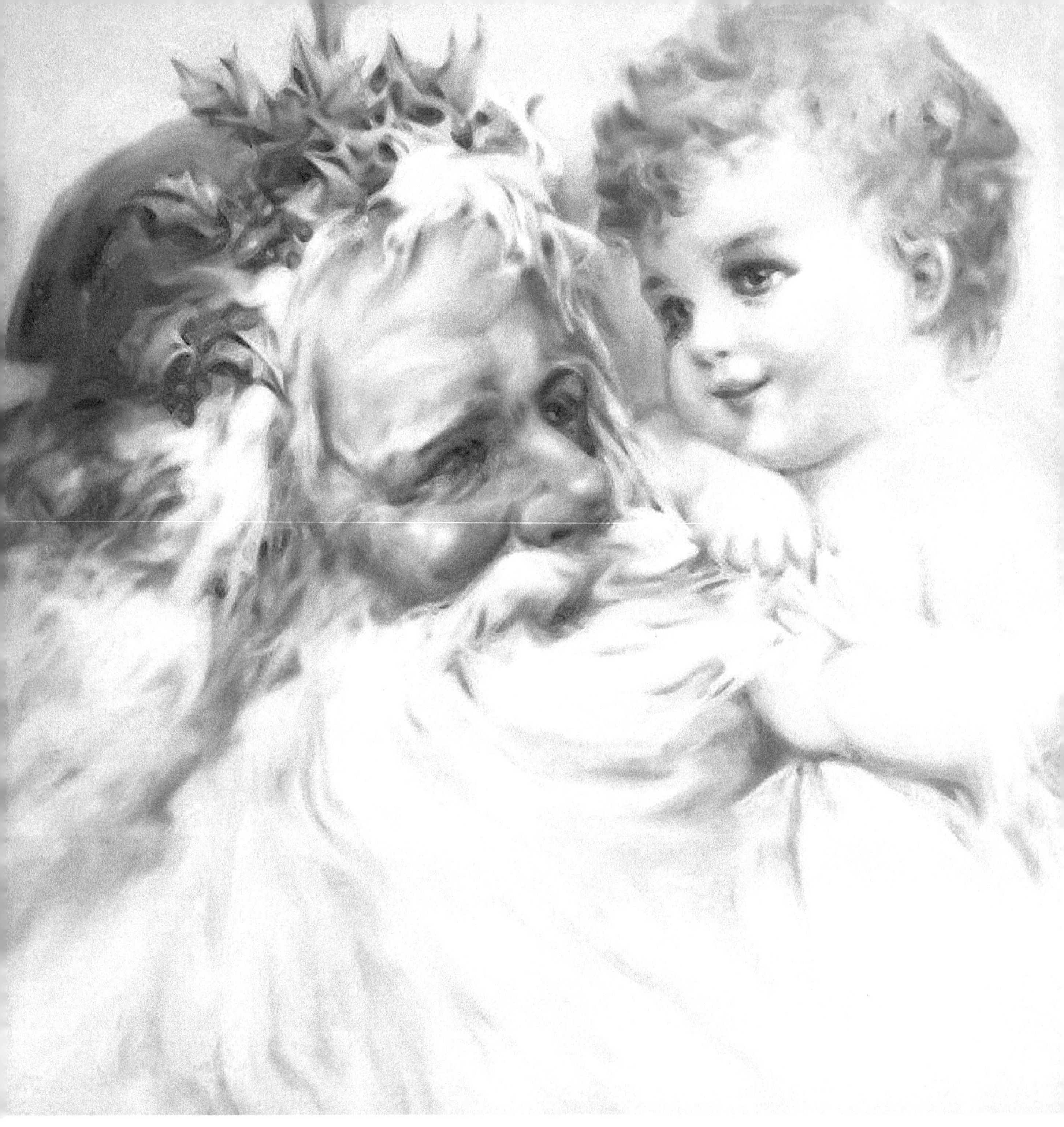

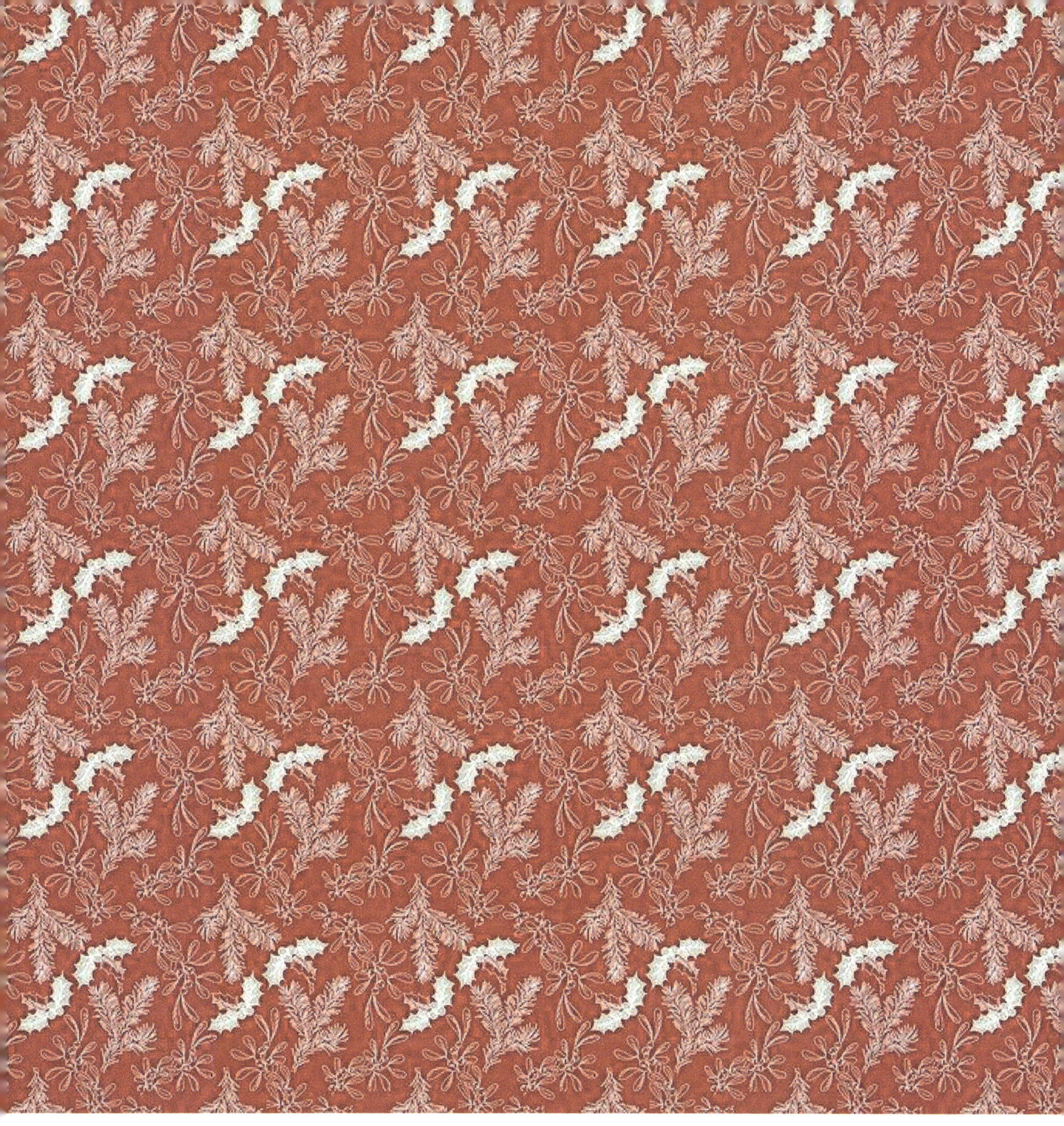

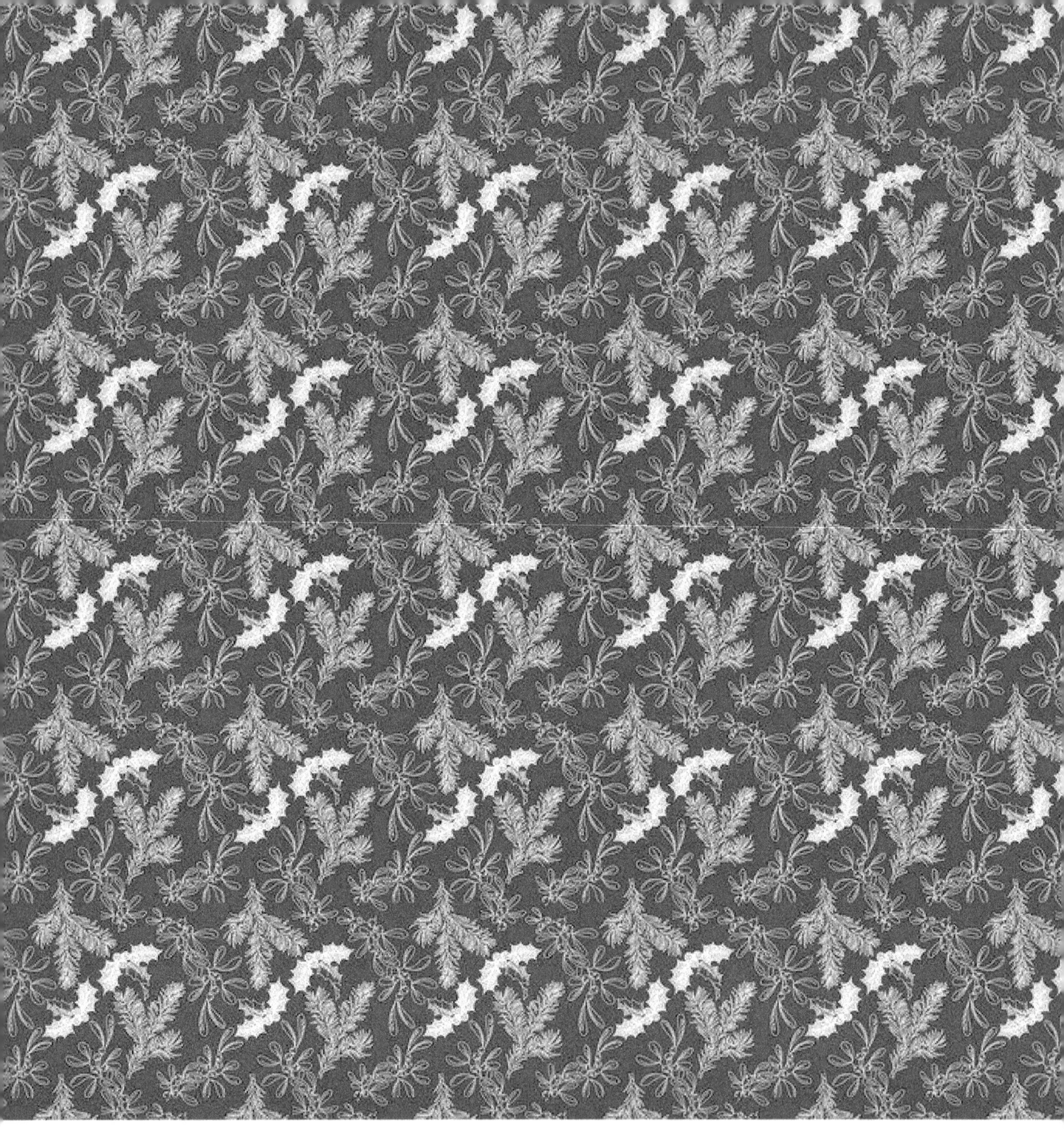

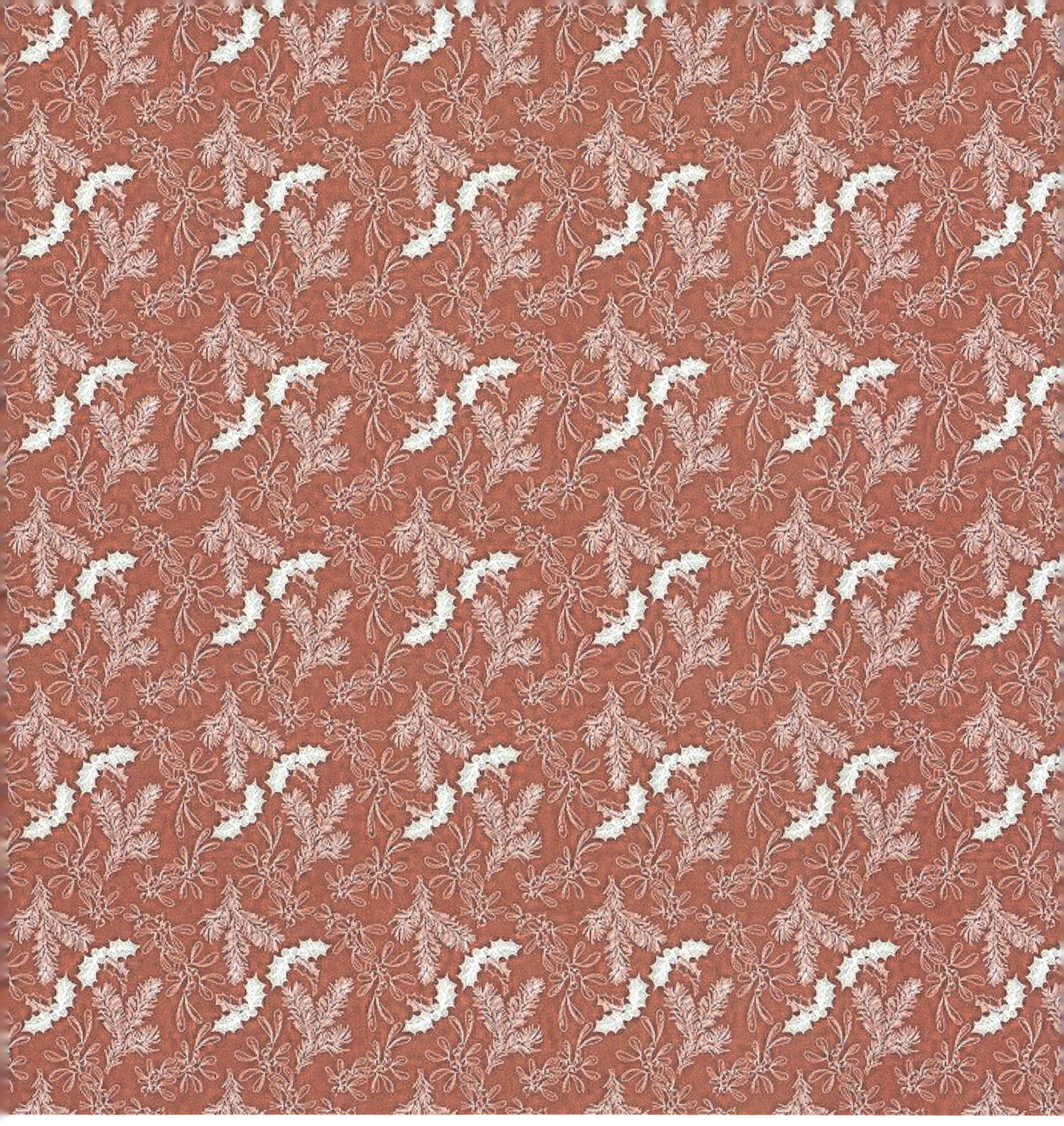

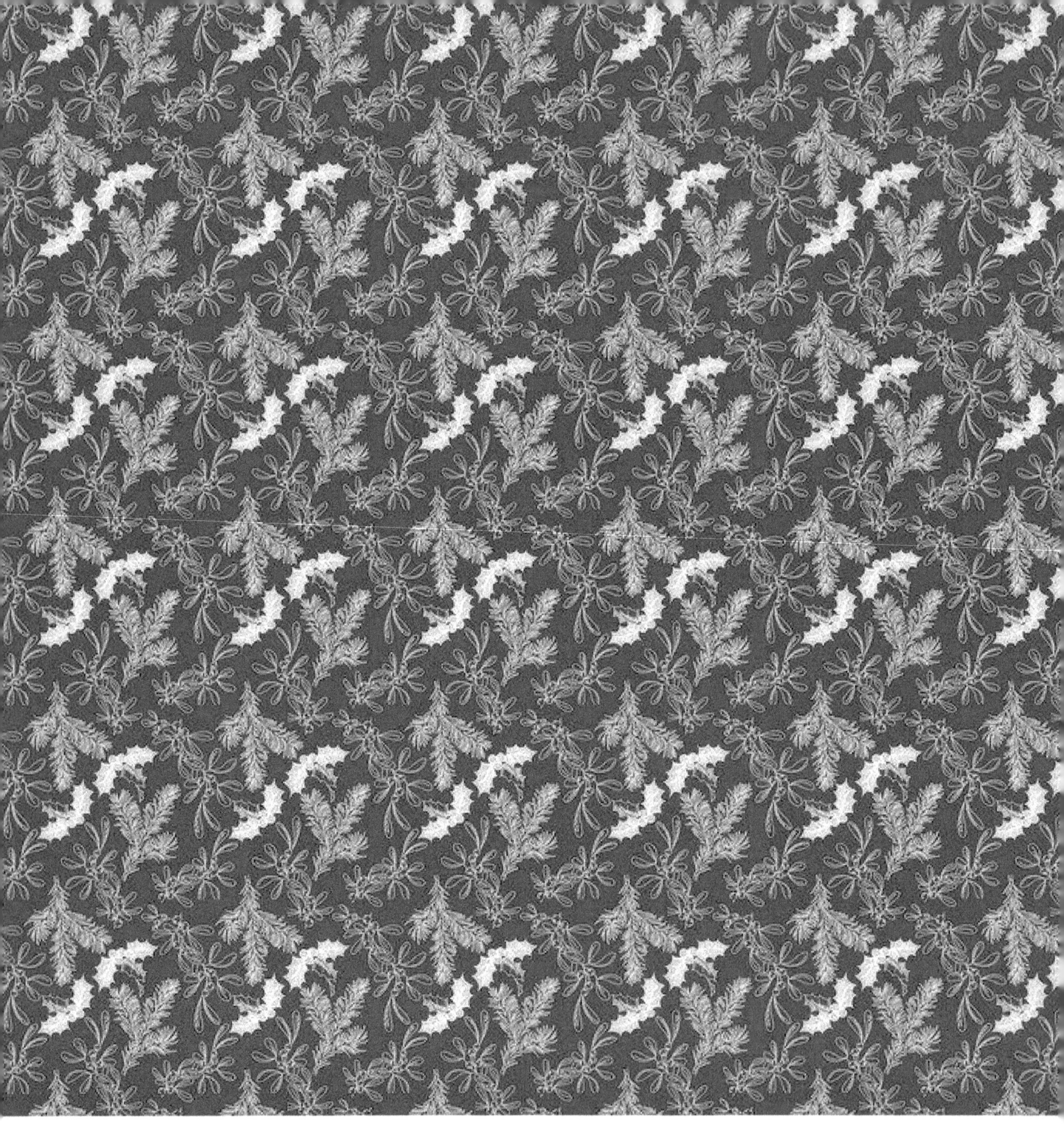